SCHOLASTIC

ADDITION & SUBTRACTION

by Susan Dillon

New York • Toronto • London • Auckland • Sydney
Mexico City • New Delhi • Hong Kong • Buenos Aires

Teaching *Resources*

A great big thanks to . . .

- teacher Ms. Donna Del Guercio for her big help in the creation of this book

- the Math for Laughs "activity testers"

- everyone in Maplewood Community Music, the t'bone four, and my esteemed teacher for the music, friendship, love

- Liam for his love of robots, Jackson for his love of math, and Luke for his love of pretty much everything

Cover design by Jannie Ho

Interior design by Ellen Matlach for Boultinghouse & Boultinghouse, Inc.

Interior illustrations by Teresa Anderko

ISBN-13 978-0-439-54885-4
ISBN-10 0-439-54885-3

Contents

Introduction

It's a fact: Students need to know their math facts! According to the Principles and Standards for School Mathematics published by the National Council on the Teaching of Mathematics (NCTM), fluency is a goal of grades 1 and 2: "By *fluency* we mean that students are able to compute efficiently and accurately with single-digit numbers." One way to achieve this fluency is to practice.

Inspired by my fifth-grade son and my work with elementary-age children, I created *Fast Facts* based on the idea that students love a race. Whether it's a friendly game with classmates or measuring their own self-improvement, students get pumped up for practice when you throw in a little healthy competition as incentive.

This book contains reproducible activity sheets to reinforce your lessons and get students on track to faster mental computation of addition and subtraction facts. Each section includes four sheets. The first one is easiest (rated level 1), the second is more difficult (level 2), and the third contains the most difficult problems (level 3). The last features blanks that you can fill in with any problems you choose. All activity sheets contain 18 problems.

Knowing math facts is a key building block to advanced math, and to a lifetime of mental math competency. NCTM states: "Ambitious standards are required to achieve a society that has the capability to think and reason mathematically. . . ." From tallying a grocery bill to estimating the mileage of the drive to the store—without a calculator—students will use these skills for the rest of their lives.

So . . . have fun with the fast facts!

Racetrack

How can students see and celebrate improvement? There are several ways students can track their speed and accuracy as you use certain favorite activity sheets from this book again and again.

To improve students' facts calculations, assign the same activity sheet every day for three days or more as classwork or homework. Make plenty of photocopies! Let students keep track of their own improvement with the Racetrack on page 7.

 ## Speed

Before beginning the activity sheet, students should go to the stopwatch icon, located at the bottom left corner of the activity sheet. Direct students to fill in the number of minutes and seconds they will have to solve the problems. You can take care of the timing. Students will complete as many problems accurately as possible. There are different ways you can approach this. For example, if you start the activity with 10 minutes to complete the sheet, each time you revisit the same activity, you can reduce the amount of allotted time gradually. Or, if you start the activity with 1 minute, each time you revisit the activity, students can try to increase the number of problems they can solve in that time.

 ## Accuracy

Emphasize that while the goal is for work to be done quickly it must also be done accurately. Each activity sheet has a bull's eye at the bottom right corner. This area is for recording the accuracy of the work done (the total answers minus the incorrect answers equals the correct answers). You can fill in this section, or students can grade their own sheets while you call out the correct answers from the answer key (page 48). Depending on the needs of your students, you can also create and display an answer key for individual activity sheets by filling in the answers and copying the completed sheet onto an overhead transparency.

Assessment

Even the youngest students can maintain their own Racetrack (page 7) with some guidance. They can judge for themselves if they were faster and/or more accurate than the last race. Ask them to compare their speed and accuracy for this race with the last race: "Did you get more answers right this time?" Or, pointing to the time, ask: "Do you think this number is smaller than this number? If so, that means you were faster!" Feel free to urge students who experience a one-time nose-dive in speed or accuracy to try a race again. After completing the required races, ask students: "How did you do?" Let them answer in their own words.

Challenge

Note that activity sheets in each section gradually increase in difficulty depending on grade-appropriate content. You may want to skip to more challenging sheets for older students. Keep in mind though that the easiest sheets are great speed practice for even the most advanced students. Since the activity sheets have 18 problems, consider cutting some problems for the youngest students. When revisiting an activity sheet multiple times, you can make it different and more challenging by asking students to complete answers right to left, bottom to top, or starting somewhere in the middle of the activity (for instance, "start at the letter *d*"). Use the blank sheet to write problems that are better geared toward your lessons.

Motivation

Photocopy and distribute at least one copy per student of the racetrack on page 7. Students should write their name in the space provided on the racetrack, along with the name of the activity sheet they will use. Students also get a new copy of a racer icon each time they complete an activity sheet. On the icon, they should write Race 1, Race 2, Race 3, and so on. Choose from the reproducible samples on page 6 or have students draw their own. A racer begins on the starting line (attach to individual tracks with tape).

The track is divided into 18 segments, matching the number of problems on the activity sheet. Students can indicate their progress by attaching a racer to the segment that represents the number of problems they solved accurately within an allotted time. The goal is to increase this number, getting closer to the finish line (18 correct answers).

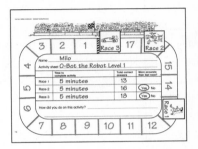

The number of segments you include can also relate to the number of times you plan to use a certain sheet. For example, if you direct students to complete the "O-Bot the Robot Level 1" sheet three times in three days, the track could be divided into thirds. In this case, students only use one copy of a racer icon. If a student improves timing and/or accuracy, she or he should take the racer and put it in the next segment on the track, advancing toward the finish.

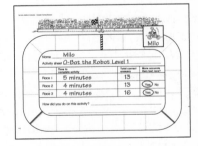

Either way you approach the activities, encourage students' improvement with medals! You can buy these at any party goods store. Or, use the reproducible version on page 6 and attach directly to students' shirts with tape, or with a safety pin attached to the back of the cut-out with masking tape. Using a rubber stamp with a simple, positive saying such as "Great effort!" or "Wow!" is also an effective way to motivate students or acknowledge their improvement.

Fast Facts: Addition & Subtraction   Scholastic Teaching Resources

Name _____

Activity sheet _____

	Time to complete activity	Total correct answers	More accurate than last race?
Race 1			
Race 2			Yes No
Race 3			Yes No

How did you do on this activity? _____

Name _____ Date _____

Easy as 1-2-3

Addition is as easy as 1, 2, and 3! Solve the problems below.
Try to get those facts fast!

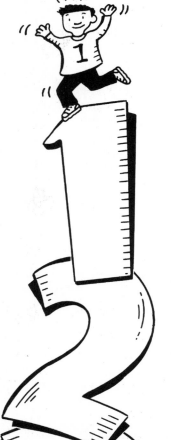

a. $0 + 2 =$ _____

b. $3 + 1 =$ _____

c. $0 + 5 =$ _____

d. $3 + 3 =$ _____

e. $2 + 4 =$ _____

f. $1 + 3 =$ _____

g. $4 + 0 =$ _____

h. $1 + 5 =$ _____

i. $3 + 2 =$ _____

j. $1 + 2 =$ _____

k. $5 + 1 =$ _____

l. $0 + 7 =$ _____

m. $3 + 4 =$ _____

n. $4 + 0 =$ _____

o. $1 + 4 =$ _____

p. $4 + 3 =$ _____

q. $3 + 5 =$ _____

r. $2 + 3 =$ _____

★ **Record your time and correct answers** ★
on your Racetrack chart.

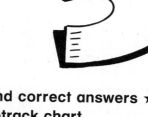

Time to complete:

_____ minutes _____ seconds

Total answers: _____

Incorrect answers: _____

Correct answers: _____

8

Easy as 1-2-3

Addition is as easy as 1, 2, and 3! Solve the problems below.
Try to get those facts fast!

a. 7 + 2 = _____

b. 5 + 5 = _____

c. 3 + 6 = _____

d. 5 + 7 = _____

e. 8 + 5 = _____

f. 3 + 8 = _____

g. 5 + 6 = _____

h. 8 + 3 = _____

i. 9 + 5 = _____

j. 6 + 6 = _____

k. 2 + 9 = _____

l. 4 + 7 = _____

m. 9 + 3 = _____

n. 7 + 4 = _____

o. 4 + 6 = _____

p. 2 + 7 = _____

q. 6 + 5 = _____

r. 9 + 4 = _____

★ **Record your time and correct answers** ★
on your Racetrack chart.

Time to complete:

_____ minutes _____ seconds

Total answers: _____

Incorrect answers: _____

Correct answers: _____

Easy as 1-2-3

Addition is as easy as 1, 2, and 3! Solve the problems below.
Try to get those facts fast!

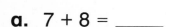

a. 7 + 8 = _____

b. 9 + 9 = _____

c. 4 + 8 = _____

d. 8 + 5 = _____

e. 6 + 6 = _____

f. 8 + 8 = _____

g. 9 + 7 = _____

h. 5 + 9 = _____

i. 6 + 7 = _____

j. 8 + 4 = _____

k. 5 + 6 = _____

l. 6 + 8 = _____

m. 7 + 5 = _____

n. 6 + 9 = _____

o. 9 + 8 = _____

p. 4 + 9 = _____

q. 7 + 7 = _____

r. 5 + 8 = _____

★ **Record your time and correct answers** ★
on your Racetrack chart.

Time to complete:

_____ minutes _____ seconds

Total answers: _____

Incorrect answers: _____

Correct answers: _____

Easy as 1-2-3

Addition is as easy as 1, 2, and 3! Solve the problems below.
Try to get those facts fast!

a. __ + __ = ____

b. __ + __ = ____

c. __ + __ = ____

d. __ + __ = ____

e. __ + __ = ____

f. __ + __ = ____

g. __ + __ = ____

h. __ + __ = ____

i. __ + __ = ____

j. __ + __ = ____

k. __ + __ = ____

l. __ + __ = ____

m. __ + __ = ____

n. __ + __ = ____

o. __ + __ = ____

p. __ + __ = ____

q. __ + __ = ____

r. __ + __ = ____

★ **Record your time and correct answers ★
on your Racetrack chart.**

Time to complete:

_____ minutes _____ seconds

Total answers: _____

Incorrect answers: _____

Correct answers: _____

O-Bot the Robot

O-Bot is a special robot made with math! Solve the problems to build the robot from head to toe. **Try to get those facts fast!**

a. $2 + 2 =$ _____

b. $1 + 4 =$ _____

c. $4 + 2 =$ _____

d. $1 + 2 =$ _____

e. $5 + 0 =$ _____

f. $2 + 4 =$ _____

g. $3 + 3 =$ _____

h. $2 + 1 =$ _____

i. $1 + 5 =$ _____

j. $0 + 4 =$ _____

k. $4 + 1 =$ _____

l. $3 + 2 =$ _____

m. $3 + 4 =$ _____

n. $5 + 1 =$ _____

o. $1 + 7 =$ _____

p. $3 + 5 =$ _____

q. $4 + 3 =$ _____

r. $5 + 2 =$ _____

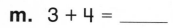

★ **Record your time and correct answers** ★
on your Racetrack chart.

Time to complete:

_____ minutes _____ seconds

Total answers: _____

Incorrect answers: _____

Correct answers: _____

Name _____ Date _____

O-Bot the Robot

O-Bot is a special robot made with math! Solve the problems to build the robot from head to toe. **Try to get those facts fast!**

a. $2 + 6 =$ _____

b. $3 + 7 =$ _____

c. $5 + 6 =$ _____

d. $8 + 2 =$ _____

e. $7 + 4 =$ _____

f. $5 + 5 =$ _____

g. $9 + 3 =$ _____

h. $4 + 6 =$ _____

i. $8 + 3 =$ _____

j. $2 + 9 =$ _____

k. $8 + 4 =$ _____

l. $5 + 7 =$ _____

m. $6 + 6 =$ _____

n. $9 + 5 =$ _____

o. $4 + 8 =$ _____

p. $7 + 6 =$ _____

q. $3 + 8 =$ _____

r. $7 + 5 =$ _____

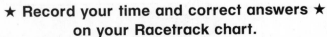
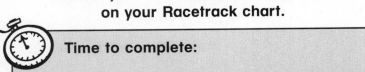

★ **Record your time and correct answers** ★
on your Racetrack chart.

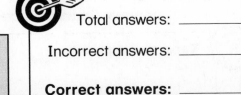

Time to complete:

_____ minutes _____ seconds

Total answers: _____

Incorrect answers: _____

Correct answers: _____

Name _____ Date _____

O-Bot the Robot

O-Bot is a special robot made with math! Solve the problems to build the robot from head to toe. **Try to get those facts fast!**

a. 6 + 8 = _____

b. 5 + 6 = _____

c. 8 + 7 = _____

d. 4 + 9 = _____

e. 8 + 4 = _____

f. 5 + 9 = _____

g. 8 + 8 = _____

h. 6 + 5 = _____

i. 6 + 9 = _____

j. 7 + 7 = _____

k. 8 + 6 = _____

l. 9 + 9 = _____

m. 9 + 6 = _____

n. 6 + 6 = _____

o. 4 + 8 = _____

p. 9 + 7 = _____

q. 8 + 9 = _____

r. 8 + 5 = _____

★ **Record your time and correct answers** ★
on your Racetrack chart.

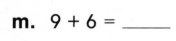

Time to complete:

_____ minutes _____ seconds

Total answers: _____

Incorrect answers: _____

Correct answers: _____

14

Fast Facts: Addition & Subtraction Scholastic Teaching Resources

Name _____ Date _____

O-Bot the Robot

O-Bot is a special robot made with math! Solve the problems to build the robot from head to toe. **Try to get those facts fast!**

a. __ + __ = _____

b. __ + __ = _____

c. __ + __ = _____

d. __ + __ = _____

e. __ + __ = _____

f. __ + __ = _____

g. __ + __ = _____

h. __ + __ = _____

i. __ + __ = _____

j. __ + __ = _____

k. __ + __ = _____

l. __ + __ = _____

m. __ + __ = _____

n. __ + __ = _____

o. __ + __ = _____

p. __ + __ = _____

q. __ + __ = _____

r. __ + __ = _____

★ **Record your time and correct answers** ★
on your Racetrack chart.

Time to complete:

_____ minutes _____ seconds

Total answers: _____

Incorrect answers: _____

Correct answers: _____

Fast Facts: Addition & Subtraction Scholastic Teaching Resources

Name _____   Date _____

Addition Steeplechase

Ride through the course without a spill by solving the problems.
Put the answers on the rider's back. **Try to get those facts fast!**

a. $5 + 2 =$ _____

b. $2 + 4 =$ _____

f. $5 + 0 =$ _____

g. $1 + 3 =$ _____

h. $2 + 1 =$ _____

c. $1 + 7 =$ _____

d. $2 + 2 =$ _____

e. $4 + 3 =$ _____

i. $4 + 0 =$ _____

j. $0 + 8 =$ _____

k. $2 + 5 =$ _____

l. $3 + 3 =$ _____

m. $1 + 4 =$ _____

n. $2 + 3 =$ _____

o. $0 + 6 =$ _____

p. $1 + 5 =$ _____

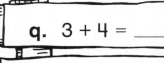

q. $3 + 4 =$ _____

r. $4 + 2 =$ _____

★ **Record your time and correct answers** ★
on your Racetrack chart.

Time to complete:

_____ minutes _____ seconds

Total answers: _____

Incorrect answers: _____

Correct answers:

Fast Facts: Addition & Subtraction Scholastic Teaching Resources

Name _____   Date _____

Addition Steeplechase

LEVEL 2

Ride through the course without a spill by solving the problems.
Put the answers on the rider's back. **Try to get those facts fast!**

a. 5 + 5 = _____

b. 2 + 9 = _____

f. 8 + 5 = _____

g. 5 + 6 = _____

h. 2 + 8 = _____

c. 7 + 4 = _____

d. 8 + 2 = _____

e. 3 + 5 = _____

i. 4 + 6 = _____

j. 8 + 4 = _____

k. 9 + 3 = _____

l. 2 + 7 = _____

m. 4 + 8 = _____

n. 6 + 3 = _____

o. 6 + 5 = _____

p. 9 + 4 = _____

q. 3 + 9 = _____

r. 6 + 4 = _____

★ **Record your time and correct answers** ★
on your Racetrack chart.

Total answers: _____

Incorrect answers: _____

Time to complete:

_____ minutes _____ seconds

Correct answers: _____

Fast Facts: Addition & Subtraction   Scholastic Teaching Resources

Name _____   Date _____

Addition Steeplechase

Ride through the course without a spill by solving the problems.
Put the answers on the rider's back. **Try to get those facts fast!**

a. $7 + 9 =$ _____

b. $4 + 8 =$ _____

c. $6 + 5 =$ _____

d. $8 + 4 =$ _____

e. $9 + 6 =$ _____

f. $5 + 9 =$ _____

g. $9 + 7 =$ _____

h. $5 + 8 =$ _____

i. $7 + 6 =$ _____

j. $8 + 8 =$ _____

k. $7 + 5 =$ _____

l. $7 + 7 =$ _____

m. $8 + 9 =$ _____

n. $6 + 7 =$ _____

o. $4 + 9 =$ _____

p. $6 + 8 =$ _____

q. $9 + 9 =$ _____

r. $5 + 7 =$ _____

★ **Record your time and correct answers** ★
on your Racetrack chart.

Time to complete:

_____ minutes _____ seconds

Total answers: _____

Incorrect answers: _____

Correct answers: _____

18

Name _____ Date _____

Addition Steeplechase

Ride through the course without a spill by solving the problems.
Put the answers on the rider's back. **Try to get those facts fast!**

a. __ + __ = ____

b. __ + __ = ____

c. __ + __ = ____

d. __ + __ = ____

e. __ + __ = ____

f. __ + __ = ____

g. __ + __ = ____

h. __ + __ = ____

i. __ + __ = ____

j. __ + __ = ____

k. __ + __ = ____

l. __ + __ = ____

m. __ + __ = ____

n. __ + __ = ____

o. __ + __ = ____

p. __ + __ = ____

q. __ + __ = ____

r. __ + __ = ____

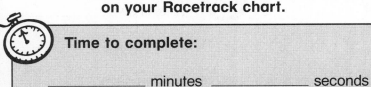

★ **Record your time and correct answers** ★
on your Racetrack chart.

Time to complete:

_____ minutes _____ seconds

Total answers: _____

Incorrect answers: _____

Correct answers: _____

Fast Facts: Addition & Subtraction Scholastic Teaching Resources

Name _____ Date _____

Space Race

Solve the problems below and you'll be a "star"!
Try to get those facts fast!

a. 3 + 5 = _____

b. 0 + 9 = _____

c. 4 + 1 = _____

d. 2 + 4 = _____

e. 5 + 2 = _____

f. 0 + 5 = _____

g. 3 + 3 = _____

h. 1 + 4 = _____

i. 5 + 1 = _____

j. 2 + 5 = _____

k. 1 + 8 = _____

n. 4 + 2 = _____

o. 1 + 6 = _____

p. 3 + 1 = _____

l. 4 + 3 = _____

m. 2 + 2 = _____

q. 0 + 7 = _____

r. 2 + 3 = _____

★ **Record your time and correct answers** ★
on your Racetrack chart.

Total answers: _____

Incorrect answers: _____

Time to complete:

_____ minutes _____ seconds

Correct answers: _____

20

Fast Facts: Addition & Subtraction Scholastic Teaching Resources

Name _____ Date _____

Space Race

Solve the problems below and you'll be a "star"!
Try to get those facts fast!

a. 8 + 3 = _____

b. 6 + 4 = _____

c. 2 + 6 = _____

d. 4 + 8 = _____

e. 9 + 3 = _____

f. 5 + 5 = _____

g. 8 + 4 = _____

h. 2 + 7 = _____

i. 5 + 7 = _____

n. 6 + 6 = _____

o. 8 + 5 = _____

j. 7 + 4 = _____

k. 9 + 4 = _____

p. 3 + 8 = _____

q. 4 + 6 = _____

l. 2 + 8 = _____

m. 3 + 7 = _____

r. 2 + 9 = _____

★ **Record your time and correct answers** ★
on your Racetrack chart.

Time to complete:

_____ minutes _____ seconds

Total answers: _____

Incorrect answers: _____

Correct answers: _____

Fast Facts: Addition & Subtraction   Scholastic Teaching Resources

Name _____ Date _____

Space Race

Solve the problems below and you'll be a "star"!

Try to get those facts fast!

a. 9 + 6 = _____

b. 6 + 5 = _____

c. 4 + 7 = _____

d. 7 + 7 = _____

e. 8 + 5 = _____

f. 5 + 6 = _____

g. 7 + 9 = _____

h. 9 + 8 = _____

i. 4 + 8 = _____

j. 6 + 6 = _____

k. 9 + 9 = _____

n. 6 + 7 = _____

o. 8 + 8 = _____

p. 6 + 9 = _____

q. 4 + 6 = _____

l. 5 + 9 = _____

m. 8 + 4 = _____

r. 7 + 6 = _____

★ **Record your time and correct answers** ★
on your Racetrack chart.

Time to complete:

_____ minutes _____ seconds

Total answers: _____

Incorrect answers: _____

Correct answers:

22

Name _____ Date _____

Space Race

Solve the problems below and you'll be a "star"!
Try to get those facts fast!

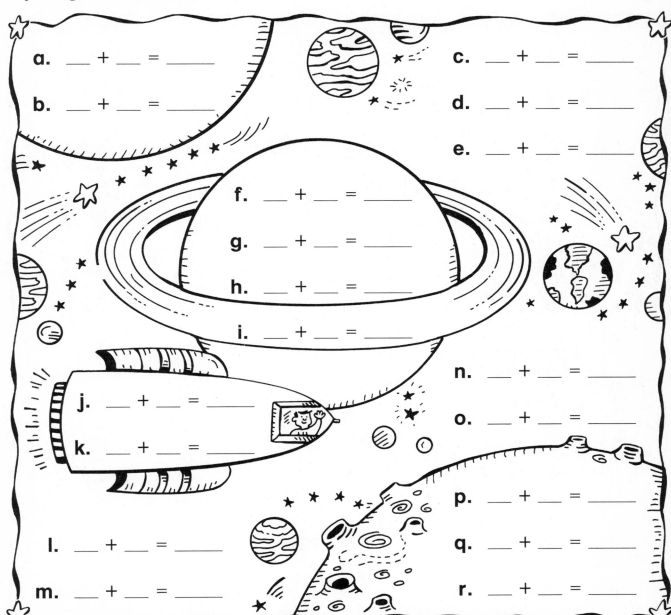

a. ___ + ___ = _____

b. ___ + ___ = _____

c. ___ + ___ = _____

d. ___ + ___ = _____

e. ___ + ___ = _____

f. ___ + ___ = _____

g. ___ + ___ = _____

h. ___ + ___ = _____

i. ___ + ___ = _____

j. ___ + ___ = _____

k. ___ + ___ = _____

l. ___ + ___ = _____

m. ___ + ___ = _____

n. ___ + ___ = _____

o. ___ + ___ = _____

p. ___ + ___ = _____

q. ___ + ___ = _____

r. ___ + ___ = _____

★ **Record your time and correct answers** ★
on your Racetrack chart.

Time to complete:

_____ minutes _____ seconds

Total answers: _____

Incorrect answers: _____

Correct answers: _____

Fast Facts: Addition & Subtraction Scholastic Teaching Resources

Name _____ Date _____

Sub-Sea Adventure

What do you see in the deep blue sea? Solve the problems below.
Try to get those facts fast!

a. $5 - 1 =$ _____

b. $3 - 2 =$ _____

c. $2 - 1 =$ _____

d. $5 - 2 =$ _____

e. $4 - 3 =$ _____

f. $6 - 0 =$ _____

g. $3 - 1 =$ _____

h. $5 - 4 =$ _____

i. $4 - 2 =$ _____

j. $7 - 0 =$ _____

k. $2 - 2 =$ _____

l. $6 - 5 =$ _____

m. $3 - 3 =$ _____

n. $6 - 1 =$ _____

o. $9 - 0 =$ _____

p. $7 - 1 =$ _____

q. $7 - 2 =$ _____

r. $5 - 5 =$ _____

★ **Record your time and correct answers** ★
on your Racetrack chart.

Time to complete:

_____ minutes _____ seconds

Total answers: _____

Incorrect answers: _____

Correct answers: _____

24

Name _____ Date _____

Sub-Sea Adventure

What do you see in the deep blue sea? Solve the problems below.
Try to get those facts fast!

a. $8 - 3 =$ _____

b. $7 - 4 =$ _____

c. $11 - 7 =$ _____

d. $12 - 3 =$ _____

e. $8 - 4 =$ _____

f. $9 - 7 =$ _____

g. $9 - 3 =$ _____

h. $12 - 5 =$ _____

i. $6 - 4 =$ _____

j. $8 - 2 =$ _____

k. $9 - 4 =$ _____

l. $13 - 4 =$ _____

m. $10 - 6 =$ _____

n. $11 - 8 =$ _____

o. $8 - 4 =$ _____

p. $7 - 3 =$ _____

q. $13 - 5 =$ _____

r. $9 - 6 =$ _____

★ **Record your time and correct answers** ★
on your Racetrack chart.

Time to complete:

_____ minutes _____ seconds

Total answers: _____

Incorrect answers: _____

Correct answers: _____

Name _____ Date _____

Sub-Sea Adventure

What do you see in the deep blue sea? Solve the problems below.
Try to get those facts fast!

a. $16 - 8 =$ _____

b. $15 - 6 =$ _____

c. $12 - 7 =$ _____

d. $18 - 9 =$ _____

e. $14 - 8 =$ _____

f. $13 - 6 =$ _____

g. $16 - 7 =$ _____

h. $17 - 9 =$ _____

i. $16 - 9 =$ _____

j. $14 - 7 =$ _____

k. $10 - 5 =$ _____

l. $13 - 8 =$ _____

m. $14 - 6 =$ _____

n. $15 - 8 =$ _____

o. $14 - 9 =$ _____

p. $11 - 6 =$ _____

q. $13 - 7 =$ _____

r. $17 - 8 =$ _____

★ **Record your time and correct answers** ★
on your Racetrack chart.

Time to complete:

_____ minutes _____ seconds

Total answers: _____

Incorrect answers: _____

Correct answers: _____

Fast Facts: Addition & Subtraction Scholastic Teaching Resources

Sub-Sea Adventure

What do you see in the deep blue sea? Solve the problems below.
Try to get those facts fast!

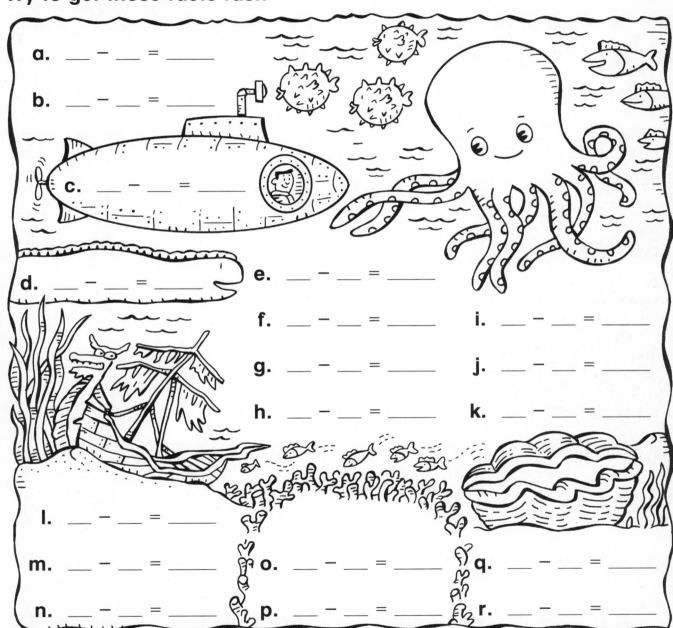

a. ___ − ___ = ___

b. ___ − ___ = ___

c. ___ − ___ = ___

d. ___ − ___ = ___

e. ___ − ___ = ___

f. ___ − ___ = ___

g. ___ − ___ = ___

h. ___ − ___ = ___

i. ___ − ___ = ___

j. ___ − ___ = ___

k. ___ − ___ = ___

l. ___ − ___ = ___

m. ___ − ___ = ___

n. ___ − ___ = ___

o. ___ − ___ = ___

p. ___ − ___ = ___

q. ___ − ___ = ___

r. ___ − ___ = ___

★ **Record your time and correct answers** ★
on your Racetrack chart.

Time to complete:

_____ minutes _____ seconds

Total answers: _____

Incorrect answers: _____

Correct answers: _____

Name _____ Date _____

Downhill Ski

You're skiing in a big race. To win, solve the problems below.
Try to get those facts fast!

a. $7 - 4 =$ _____

b. $6 - 2 =$ _____

c. $3 - 3 =$ _____

d. $10 - 9 =$ _____

e. $8 - 0 =$ _____

f. $11 - 2 =$ _____

g. $4 - 3 =$ _____

h. $7 - 5 =$ _____

i. $8 - 7 =$ _____

j. $8 - 5 =$ _____

k. $6 - 0 =$ _____

l. $4 - 4 =$ _____

m. $9 - 2 =$ _____

n. $8 - 1 =$ _____

o. $6 - 6 =$ _____

p. $7 - 2 =$ _____

q. $5 - 3 =$ _____

r. $10 - 2 =$ _____

★ **Record your time and correct answers** ★
on your Racetrack chart.

Time to complete:

_____ minutes _____ seconds

Total answers: _____

Incorrect answers: _____

Correct answers: _____

28

Fast Facts: Addition & Subtraction Scholastic Teaching Resources

Name _____   Date _____

Downhill Ski

You're skiing in a big race. To win, solve the problems below.
Try to get those facts fast!

a. $12 - 8 =$ _____

b. $9 - 6 =$ _____

c. $8 - 4 =$ _____

d. $11 - 9 =$ _____

e. $11 - 4 =$ _____

f. $13 - 9 =$ _____

g. $12 - 3 =$ _____

k. $7 - 3 =$ _____

l. $10 - 8 =$ _____

m. $7 - 4 =$ _____

n. $9 - 4 =$ _____

o. $11 - 3 =$ _____

h. $14 - 5 =$ _____

i. $10 - 6 =$ _____

j. $12 - 4 =$ _____

p. $8 - 6 =$ _____

q. $10 - 7 =$ _____

r. $11 - 3 =$ _____

★ **Record your time and correct answers** ★
on your Racetrack chart.

Time to complete:

_____ minutes _____ seconds

Total answers: _____

Incorrect answers: _____

Correct answers: _____

Fast Facts: Addition & Subtraction Scholastic Teaching Resources

Name _____ Date _____

Downhill Ski

You're skiing in a big race. To win, solve the problems below.
Try to get those facts fast!

a. $17 - 8 =$ _____

b. $12 - 7 =$ _____

c. $13 - 5 =$ _____

d. $15 - 8 =$ _____

e. $16 - 9 =$ _____

f. $14 - 5 =$ _____

g. $13 - 8 =$ _____

k. $16 - 7 =$ _____

l. $11 - 6 =$ _____

m. $12 - 5 =$ _____

n. $15 - 7 =$ _____

o. $13 - 7 =$ _____

h. $18 - 9 =$ _____

i. $13 - 6 =$ _____

j. $16 - 8 =$ _____

p. $12 - 6 =$ _____

q. $14 - 8 =$ _____

r. $14 - 7 =$ _____

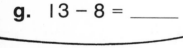

★ **Record your time and correct answers** ★
on your Racetrack chart.

Time to complete:

_____ minutes _____ seconds

Total answers: _____

Incorrect answers: _____

Correct answers: _____

30

Fast Facts: Addition & Subtraction   Scholastic Teaching Resources

Name _____   Date _____

Downhill Ski

You're skiing in a big race. To win, solve the problems below.
Try to get those facts fast!

a. ___ – ___ = ___

b. ___ – ___ = ___

c. ___ – ___ = ___

d. ___ – ___ = ___

e. ___ – ___ = ___

f. ___ – ___ = ___

g. ___ – ___ = ___

h. ___ – ___ = ___

i. ___ – ___ = ___

j. ___ – ___ = ___

k. ___ – ___ = ___

l. ___ – ___ = ___

m. ___ – ___ = ___

n. ___ – ___ = ___

o. ___ – ___ = ___

p. ___ – ___ = ___

q. ___ – ___ = ___

r. ___ – ___ = ___

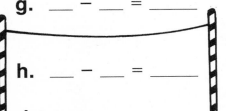

★ **Record your time and correct answers** ★
on your Racetrack chart.

Time to complete:

_____ minutes _____ seconds

Total answers: _____

Incorrect answers: _____

Correct answers: _____

31

Fast Facts: Addition & Subtraction Scholastic Teaching Resources

Fast Food

LEVEL 1

It's a huge picnic, just for you! Quick, chow down by solving the problems below. **Try to get those facts fast!**

a. $6 - 3 =$ _____

b. $10 - 1 =$ _____

c. $7 - 5 =$ _____

d. $9 - 8 =$ _____

e. $2 - 0 =$ _____

f. $8 - 2 =$ _____

g. $5 - 3 =$ _____

h. $6 - 4 =$ _____

i. $6 - 2 =$ _____

j. $7 - 6 =$ _____

k. $4 - 3 =$ _____

l. $10 - 9 =$ _____

m. $5 - 1 =$ _____

n. $7 - 2 =$ _____

o. $6 - 0 =$ _____

p. $5 - 2 =$ _____

q. $8 - 7 =$ _____

r. $9 - 0 =$ _____

★ **Record your time and correct answers** ★
on your Racetrack chart.

Time to complete:

_____ minutes _____ seconds

Total answers: _____

Incorrect answers: _____

Correct answers: _____

Fast Facts: Addition & Subtraction Scholastic Teaching Resources

Fast Food

It's a huge picnic, just for you! Quick, chow down by solving the problems below. **Try to get those facts fast!**

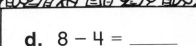

a. $13 - 4 =$ _____

b. $12 - 9 =$ _____

c. $9 - 6 =$ _____

d. $8 - 4 =$ _____

e. $10 - 3 =$ _____

f. $13 - 9 =$ _____

g. $11 - 7 =$ _____

h. $12 - 4 =$ _____

k. $11 - 3 =$ _____

l. $8 - 6 =$ _____

m. $10 - 7 =$ _____

n. $12 - 3 =$ _____

o. $8 - 5 =$ _____

p. $10 - 8 =$ _____

q. $8 - 3 =$ _____

r. $14 - 5 =$ _____

i. $9 - 3 =$ _____

j. $11 - 9 =$ _____

★ **Record your time and correct answers** ★
on your Racetrack chart.

Time to complete:

_____ minutes _____ seconds

Total answers: _____

Incorrect answers: _____

Correct answers: _____

Name _____ Date _____

Fast Food

LEVEL 3

It's a huge picnic, just for you! Quick, chow down by solving the problems below. **Try to get those facts fast!**

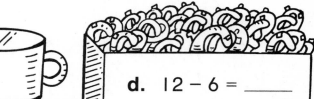

d. $12 - 6 =$ _____

e. $10 - 5 =$ _____

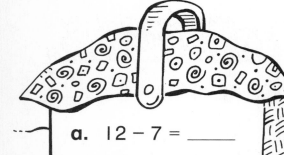

a. $12 - 7 =$ _____

b. $13 - 5 =$ _____

c. $18 - 9 =$ _____

k. $12 - 5 =$ _____

l. $16 - 9 =$ _____

f. $13 - 9 =$ _____

g. $15 - 7 =$ _____

h. $17 - 8 =$ _____

m. $15 - 6 =$ _____

n. $15 - 8 =$ _____

o. $14 - 5 =$ _____

p. $15 - 9 =$ _____

i. $14 - 7 =$ _____

j. $13 - 4 =$ _____

q. $16 - 8 =$ _____

r. $17 - 9 =$ _____

★ **Record your time and correct answers** ★
on your Racetrack chart.

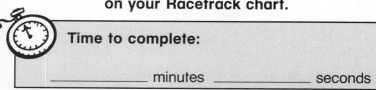

Time to complete:

_____ minutes _____ seconds

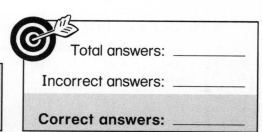

Total answers: _____

Incorrect answers: _____

Correct answers: _____

Fast Facts: Addition & Subtraction Scholastic Teaching Resources

Fast Food

It's a huge picnic, just for you! Quick, chow down by solving the problems below. **Try to get those facts fast!**

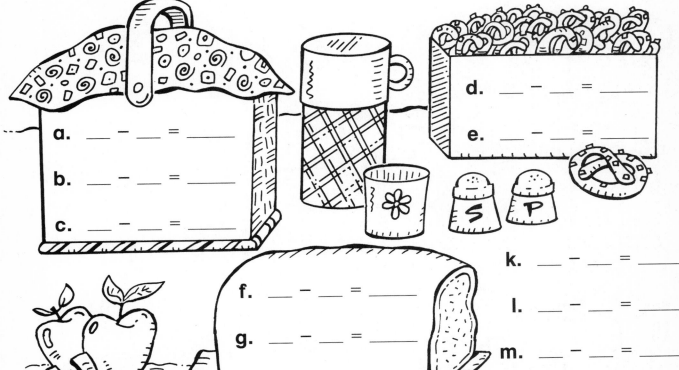

a. ___ − ___ = ___

b. ___ − ___ = ___

c. ___ − ___ = ___

d. ___ − ___ = ___

e. ___ − ___ = ___

f. ___ − ___ = ___

g. ___ − ___ = ___

h. ___ − ___ = ___

i. ___ − ___ = ___

j. ___ − ___ = ___

k. ___ − ___ = ___

l. ___ − ___ = ___

m. ___ − ___ = ___

n. ___ − ___ = ___

o. ___ − ___ = ___

p. ___ − ___ = ___

q. ___ − ___ = ___

r. ___ − ___ = ___

★ **Record your time and correct answers** ★
on your Racetrack chart.

Time to complete:

_____ minutes _____ seconds

Total answers: _____

Incorrect answers: _____

Correct answers: _____

Fast Facts: Addition & Subtraction   Scholastic Teaching Resources

LEVEL 1

Falling Leaves

Autumn is here, and leaves are falling off our favorite tree. Solve the problems before they hit the ground. **Try to get those facts fast!**

a. 2 – 2 = _____

b. 10 – 1 = _____

c. 7 – 4 = _____

d. 7 – 6 = _____

e. 9 – 8 = _____

f. 8 – 2 = _____

g. 6 – 3 = _____

h. 7 – 1 = _____

i. 4 – 0 = _____

j. 8 – 5 = _____

n. 8 – 0 = _____

o. 10 – 9 = _____

k. 6 – 2 = _____

l. 6 – 6 = _____

m. 5 – 3 = _____

p. 3 – 2 = _____

q. 7 – 5 = _____

r. 9 – 2 = _____

★ **Record your time and correct answers** ★
on your Racetrack chart.

 Time to complete:

_____ minutes _____ seconds

Total answers: _____

Incorrect answers: _____

Correct answers: _____

36

Fast Facts: Addition & Subtraction Scholastic Teaching Resources

Name _____   Date _____

Falling Leaves

Autumn is here, and leaves are falling off our favorite tree. Solve the problems before they hit the ground. **Try to get those facts fast!**

a. $10 - 6 =$ _____

b. $12 - 9 =$ _____

c. $11 - 3 =$ _____

d. $8 - 5 =$ _____

e. $10 - 3 =$ _____

f. $9 - 7 =$ _____

g. $14 - 5 =$ _____

h. $12 - 8 =$ _____

i. $6 - 3 =$ _____

j. $9 - 5 =$ _____

n. $8 - 6 =$ _____

o. $12 - 4 =$ _____

k. $10 - 7 =$ _____

l. $11 - 8 =$ _____

m. $13 - 4 =$ _____

p. $8 - 3 =$ _____

q. $11 - 4 =$ _____

r. $11 - 9 =$ _____

★ **Record your time and correct answers** ★
on your Racetrack chart.

Time to complete:

_____ minutes _____ seconds

Total answers: _____

Incorrect answers: _____

Correct answers: _____

Fast Facts: Addition & Subtraction   Scholastic Teaching Resources

LEVEL 3

Falling Leaves

Autumn is here, and leaves are falling off our favorite tree. Solve the problems before they hit the ground. **Try to get those facts fast!**

a. $13 - 7 =$ _____

b. $14 - 9 =$ _____

c. $13 - 5 =$ _____

d. $17 - 8 =$ _____

e. $12 - 6 =$ _____

f. $18 - 9 =$ _____

g. $14 - 6 =$ _____

h. $15 - 8 =$ _____

i. $12 - 7 =$ _____

j. $16 - 9 =$ _____

n. $13 - 6 =$ _____

o. $15 - 9 =$ _____

p. $14 - 5 =$ _____

q. $16 - 8 =$ _____

r. $15 - 6 =$ _____

k. $14 - 8 =$ _____

l. $17 - 9 =$ _____

m. $11 - 5 =$ _____

★ **Record your time and correct answers** ★
on your Racetrack chart.

Time to complete:

_____ minutes _____ seconds

Total answers: _____

Incorrect answers: _____

Correct answers: _____

Fast Facts: Addition & Subtraction Scholastic Teaching Resources

Name _____ Date _____

Falling Leaves

Autumn is here, and leaves are falling off our favorite tree. Solve the problems before they hit the ground. **Try to get those facts fast!**

a. ____ − ____ = ____

b. ____ − ____ = ____

c. ____ − ____ = ____

d. ____ − ____ = ____

e. ____ − ____ = ____

f. ____ − ____ = ____

g. ____ − ____ = ____

h. ____ − ____ = ____

i. ____ − ____ = ____

j. ____ − ____ = ____

k. ____ − ____ = ____

l. ____ − ____ = ____

m. ____ − ____ = ____

n. ____ − ____ = ____

o. ____ − ____ = ____

p. ____ − ____ = ____

q. ____ − ____ = ____

r. ____ − ____ = ____

★ **Record your time and correct answers** ★
on your Racetrack chart.

 Time to complete:

____ minutes ____ seconds

 Total answers: _____

Incorrect answers: _____

Correct answers: _____

Fast Facts: Addition & Subtraction   Scholastic Teaching Resources

Name _____ Date _____

A & S Airport

What a busy airport! Solve the problems below so the planes can take off and land. **Try to get those facts fast!**

a. 2 + 5 = _____

b. 10 − 2 = _____

c. 5 + 1 = _____

d. 6 − 3 = _____

e. 4 + 3 = _____

f. 7 − 4 = _____

g. 0 + 8 = _____

h. 2 − 2 = _____

i. 4 + 2 = _____

j. 5 − 4 = _____

o. 1 + 8 = _____

p. 6 − 2 = _____

k. 5 + 2 = _____

l. 7 − 2 = _____

m. 2 + 2 = _____

n. 7 − 1 = _____

q. 3 + 3 = _____

r. 7 − 5 = _____

 ★ **Record your time and correct answers** ★
on your Racetrack chart.

Time to complete:

_____ minutes _____ seconds

 Total answers: _____

Incorrect answers: _____

Correct answers: _____

40

Fast Facts: Addition & Subtraction Scholastic Teaching Resources

Name _____   Date _____

A & S Airport

What a busy airport! Solve the problems below so the planes can take off and land. **Try to get those facts fast!**

a. 3 + 6 = _____

b. 7 – 4 = _____

c. 5 + 5 = _____

d. 10 – 7 = _____

e. 8 + 2 = _____

f. 14 – 5 = _____

g. 4 + 6 = _____

h. 8 – 5 = _____

i. 7 + 4 = _____

j. 11 – 7 = _____

o. 7 + 5 = _____

p. 12 – 9 = _____

k. 6 + 6 = _____

l. 12 – 4 = _____

m. 3 + 8 = _____

n. 11 – 4 = _____

q. 9 + 2 = _____

r. 6 – 3 = _____

★ **Record your time and correct answers** ★
on your Racetrack chart.

Time to complete:

_____ minutes _____ seconds

Total answers: _____

Incorrect answers: _____

Correct answers: _____

Name _____ Date _____

A & S Airport

What a busy airport! Solve the problems below so the planes can take off and land. **Try to get those facts fast!**

a. $6 + 5 =$ _____

b. $11 - 6 =$ _____

c. $9 + 9 =$ _____

d. $15 - 6 =$ _____

e. $8 + 4 =$ _____

f. $16 - 7 =$ _____

g. $5 + 6 =$ _____

h. $12 - 7 =$ _____

i. $7 + 9 =$ _____

j. $12 - 6 =$ _____

o. $7 + 7 =$ _____

p. $13 - 6 =$ _____

k. $8 + 7 =$ _____

l. $15 - 7 =$ _____

m. $9 + 5 =$ _____

n. $18 - 9 =$ _____

q. $9 + 8 =$ _____

r. $15 - 8 =$ _____

★ **Record your time and correct answers** ★
on your Racetrack chart.

Time to complete:

_____ minutes _____ seconds

Total answers: _____

Incorrect answers: _____

Correct answers: _____

42

Fast Facts: Addition & Subtraction Scholastic Teaching Resources

Name _____ Date _____

A & S Airport

What a busy airport! Solve the problems below so the planes can take off and land. **Try to get those facts fast!**

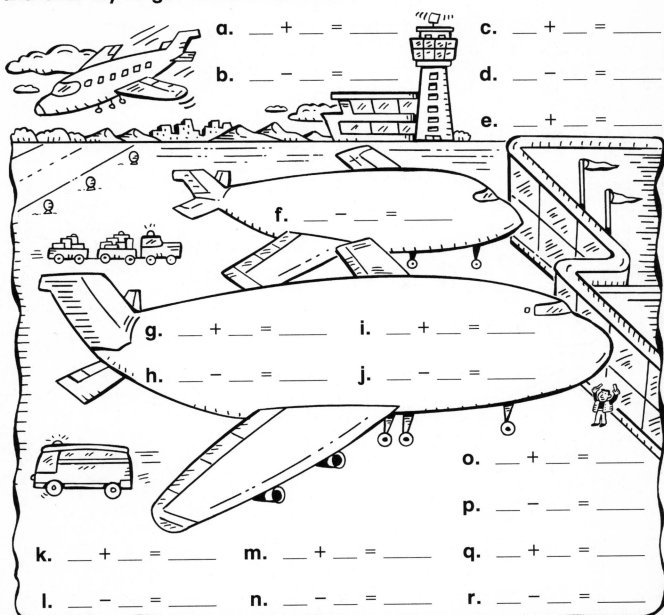

a. __ + __ = ____

b. __ − __ = ____

c. __ + __ = ____

d. __ − __ = ____

e. __ + __ = ____

f. __ − __ = ____

g. __ + __ = ____

h. __ − __ = ____

i. __ + __ = ____

j. __ − __ = ____

k. __ + __ = ____

l. __ − __ = ____

m. __ + __ = ____

n. __ − __ = ____

o. __ + __ = ____

p. __ − __ = ____

q. __ + __ = ____

r. __ − __ = ____

★ **Record your time and correct answers** ★
on your Racetrack chart.

Time to complete:

____ minutes ____ seconds

Total answers: _____

Incorrect answers: _____

Correct answers: _____

Quick Sandcastle

What a big sandcastle! Solve the problems below before the waves wash it away. **Try to get those facts fast!**

a. 5 + 1 = _____

b. 3 − 2 = _____

c. 2 + 1 = _____

d. 5 − 2 = _____

e. 4 + 3 = _____

f. 6 − 0 = _____

g. 3 + 1 = _____

h. 5 − 4 = _____

i. 4 + 2 = _____

j. 7 − 0 = _____

k. 2 + 2 = _____

l. 6 − 5 = _____

m. 3 + 3 = _____

n. 6 − 1 = _____

o. 9 + 0 = _____

p. 7 − 1 = _____

q. 7 + 2 = _____

r. 5 − 5 = _____

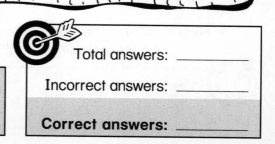

★ **Record your time and correct answers** ★
on your Racetrack chart.

Time to complete:

_____ minutes _____ seconds

Total answers: _____

Incorrect answers: _____

Correct answers: _____

44

Fast Facts: Addition & Subtraction Scholastic Teaching Resources

Name _____   Date _____

Quick Sandcastle

What a big sandcastle! Solve the problems below before the waves wash it away. **Try to get those facts fast!**

a. 3 + 8 = _____

b. 8 − 4 = _____

c. 5 + 5 = _____

d. 13 − 4 = _____

e. 6 + 3 = _____

f. 10 − 7 = _____

g. 4 + 6 = _____

h. 9 − 5 = _____

i. 2 + 7 = _____

j. 11 − 8 = _____

k. 8 + 5 = _____

l. 12 − 3 = _____

m. 4 + 6 = _____

n. 8 − 6 = _____

o. 7 + 5 = _____

p. 9 − 3 = _____

q. 5 + 6 = _____

r. 13 − 5 = _____

★ **Record your time and correct answers** ★
on your Racetrack chart.

Time to complete:

_____ minutes _____ seconds

Total answers: _____

Incorrect answers: _____

Correct answers: _____

Quick Sandcastle

LEVEL 3

What a big sandcastle! Solve the problems below before the waves wash it away. **Try to get those facts fast!**

a. $6 + 7 =$ _____

b. $14 - 5 =$ _____

c. $9 + 9 =$ _____

d. $10 - 5 =$ _____

e. $8 + 6 =$ _____

f. $14 - 7 =$ _____

g. $6 + 6 =$ _____

h. $13 - 6 =$ _____

i. $4 + 9 =$ _____

j. $15 - 8 =$ _____

k. $7 + 5 =$ _____

l. $12 - 7 =$ _____

m. $7 + 8 =$ _____

n. $18 - 9 =$ _____

o. $5 + 8 =$ _____

p. $16 - 7 =$ _____

q. $6 + 9 =$ _____

r. $14 - 6 =$ _____

★ **Record your time and correct answers** ★
on your Racetrack chart.

Time to complete:

_____ minutes _____ seconds

Total answers: _____

Incorrect answers: _____

Correct answers: _____

46

Fast Facts: Addition & Subtraction   Scholastic Teaching Resources

Name _____   Date _____

Quick Sandcastle

What a big sandcastle! Solve the problems below before the waves wash it away. **Try to get those facts fast!**

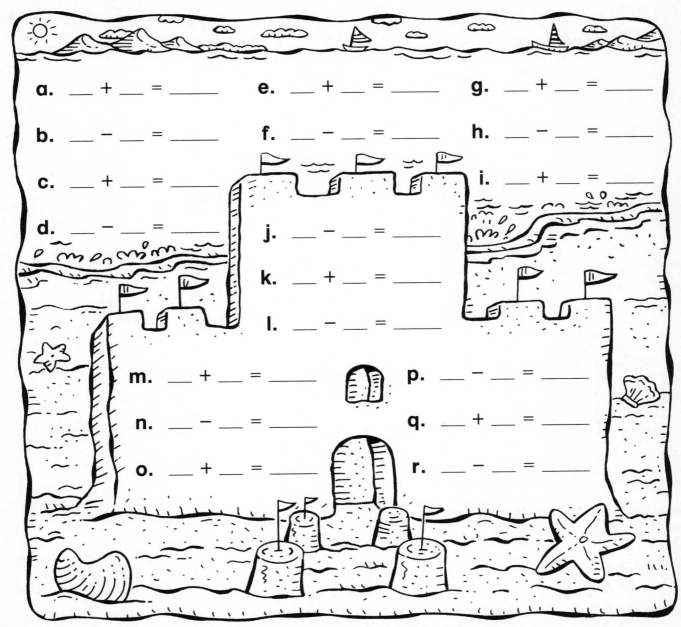

a. ___ + ___ = ___

b. ___ − ___ = ___

c. ___ + ___ = ___

d. ___ − ___ = ___

e. ___ + ___ = ___

f. ___ − ___ = ___

g. ___ + ___ = ___

h. ___ − ___ = ___

i. ___ + ___ = ___

j. ___ − ___ = ___

k. ___ + ___ = ___

l. ___ − ___ = ___

m. ___ + ___ = ___

n. ___ − ___ = ___

o. ___ + ___ = ___

p. ___ − ___ = ___

q. ___ + ___ = ___

r. ___ − ___ = ___

★ **Record your time and correct answers** ★
on your Racetrack chart.

Time to complete:

_____ minutes _____ seconds

Total answers: _____

Incorrect answers: _____

Correct answers: _____

Fast Facts: Addition & Subtraction Scholastic Teaching Resources

Answer Key

Addition

	Page 8	Page 12	Page 16	Page 20
a.	2	4	7	8
b.	4	5	6	9
c.	5	6	8	5
d.	6	3	4	6
e.	6	5	7	7
f.	4	6	5	5
g.	4	6	4	6
h.	6	3	3	5
i.	5	6	4	6
j.	3	4	8	7
k.	6	5	7	9
l.	7	5	6	7
m.	7	7	5	4
n.	4	6	5	6
o.	5	8	6	7
p.	7	8	6	4
q.	8	7	7	7
r.	5	7	6	5

	Page 9	Page 13	Page 17	Page 21
a.	9	8	10	11
b.	10	10	11	10
c.	9	11	11	8
d.	12	10	10	12
e.	13	11	8	12
f.	11	10	13	10
g.	11	12	11	12
h.	11	10	10	9
i.	14	11	10	12
j.	12	11	12	11
k.	11	12	12	13
l.	11	12	9	10
m.	12	12	12	10
n.	11	14	9	12
o.	10	12	11	13
p.	9	13	13	11
q.	11	11	12	10
r.	13	12	10	11

	Page 10	Page 14	Page 18	Page 22
a.	15	14	16	15
b.	18	11	12	11
c.	12	15	11	11
d.	13	13	12	14
e.	12	12	15	13
f.	16	14	14	11
g.	16	16	16	16
h.	14	11	13	17
i.	13	15	13	12
j.	12	14	16	12
k.	11	14	12	18
l.	14	18	14	14
m.	12	15	17	12
n.	15	12	13	13
o.	17	12	13	16
p.	13	16	14	15
q.	14	17	18	10
r.	13	13	12	13

Subtraction

	Page 24	Page 28	Page 32	Page 36
a.	4	3	3	0
b.	1	4	9	9
c.	1	0	2	3
d.	3	1	1	1
e.	1	8	2	1
f.	6	9	6	6
g.	2	1	2	3
h.	1	2	2	6
i.	2	1	4	4
j.	7	3	1	3
k.	0	6	1	4
l.	1	0	1	0
m.	0	7	4	2
n.	5	7	5	8
o.	9	0	6	1
p.	6	5	3	1
q.	5	2	1	2
r.	0	8	9	7

	Page 25	Page 29	Page 33	Page 37
a.	5	4	9	4
b.	3	3	3	3
c.	4	4	3	8
d.	9	2	4	3
e.	4	7	7	7
f.	2	4	4	2
g.	6	9	4	9
h.	7	9	8	4
i.	2	4	6	3
j.	6	8	2	4
k.	5	4	8	3
l.	9	2	2	3
m.	4	3	3	9
n.	3	5	9	2
o.	4	8	3	8
p.	4	2	2	5
q.	8	3	5	7
r.	3	8	9	2

	Page 26	Page 30	Page 34	Page 38
a.	8	9	5	6
b.	9	5	8	5
c.	5	8	9	8
d.	9	7	6	9
e.	6	7	5	6
f.	7	9	4	9
g.	9	5	8	8
h.	8	9	9	7
i.	7	7	7	5
j.	7	8	9	7
k.	5	9	7	6
l.	5	5	7	8
m.	8	7	9	6
n.	7	7	7	7
o.	5	9	9	6
p.	5	6	6	9
q.	6	7	8	8
r.	9	7	8	9

Addition/Subtraction

	Page 40	Page 44
a.	7	6
b.	8	1
c.	6	3
d.	3	3
e.	7	7
f.	3	6
g.	8	4
h.	0	1
i.	6	6
j.	1	7
k.	7	4
l.	5	1
m.	4	6
n.	6	5
o.	9	9
p.	4	6
q.	6	9
r.	2	0

	Page 41	Page 45
a.	9	11
b.	3	4
c.	8	10
d.	3	9
e.	10	9
f.	9	3
g.	10	10
h.	4	4
i.	3	9
j.	4	3
k.	3	13
l.	3	9
m.	9	10
n.	2	2
o.	8	12
p.	5	6
q.	7	11
r.	2	8

	Page 42	Page 46
a.	11	13
b.	5	9
c.	18	18
d.	9	5
e.	12	14
f.	9	7
g.	11	12
h.	5	7
i.	16	13
j.	6	7
k.	15	12
l.	8	5
m.	14	15
n.	9	9
o.	14	13
p.	7	9
q.	17	15
r.	7	8